The Isolated Jesus

Seven Messages
For Good Friday
Or Lent Based Upon
Mark's Passion Of Jesus

R. Sheldon MacKenzie

D1402280

CSS Publishing Company, Inc.
Lima, Ohio

THE ISOLATED JESUS

Library of Congress Cataloging-in-Publication Data

MacKenzie, R. Sheldon, 1930-
    The isolated Jesus : seven readings for Good Friday or Lent based on Mark's Passion narrative / R. Sheldon MacKenzie.
        p.   cm.
    ISBN 1-55673-703-3
    1. Jesus Christ—Passion—Meditations. 2. Bible. N.T. Mark XIV, 32-XV, 39—Meditations. 3. Lent—Prayer-books and devotions—English. I. Title.
BT431.M265   1994
232.96—dc20
                                                        93-39814
                                                              CIP

ISBN 1-55673-703-3   PRINTED IN U.S.A.

To

the members and friends

past and present

of

Salem Presbyterian Church

in .

Green Hill, Nova Scotia

this book

is dedicated with love and gratitude.

Table Of Contents

Introduction

The material in this booklet was developed in the first instance for use during the Three-hour Good Friday Liturgy at St. Stephen's (Episcopal) Church in Philadelphia. The invitation to present this material came from the Rev. Roy Hendricks, then Rector of St. Stephen's, to whom I owe so much for all that friendship means in terms of affection, encouragement and guidance in matters temporal and spiritual.

The passion narrative in Mark divides itself quite naturally into seven passages on which meditations may be based. Although the meditations which follow were first written and given within the context of a traditional three-hour liturgy, they may be and have been adapted for other uses during Lent generally and during Holy Week in particular.

These brief expositions have been used, for example, on a trial basis, by several Lenten study groups as a guide to the use of the Markan passion material. The reaction to this use of the material has been a positive one.

In another situation a number of meditations, selected from the seven presented here, were used during a series of special devotional acts of worship during Holy Week. They fitted easily and well into an imaginative liturgy without having either to use all seven or to make changes in the material itself.

And finally, although other uses of the material may be visualized, they might form the basis for a dramatization of these events as narrated by Mark, for use in mid-week services during Lent or at special times during Holy Week.

The emphasis on the events in the last week of Jesus' life is slightly different in Mark's gospel from the other three. In this gospel, it seems to me, the emphasis is on the process by which everyone deserted Jesus; his disciples, his own people, the religious authorities and the state. And finally, it seems that even God has left him alone.

Through the simple account in this gospel there is presented a powerful impression of Jesus rejected, humiliated, betrayed and most of all, alone and lonely. This treatment of the passion narrative in Mark is not an academic one. It is, I hope, academically sound, but it is not the intention of the reflections that follow to deal with the problems and matters of exegetical concern that would come naturally to the attention of an academic study of these passages from Mark's gospel. The intention of these brief chapters is to act as a devotional guide to those who would like to follow the passion of Jesus through the writing of one particular gospel. Having done the same some years ago for the gospel of John, this is an attempt to hear again what the earliest of the synoptic gospels had to say to his readers and to indicate in some small way what the writer has to say to us today.

Jesus
In
Gethsemane

Jesus —
Misunderstood
And Alone

1

Jesus In Gethsemane
"Jesus — Misunderstood And Alone"

Psalm 43   **Mark 14:32-42**

Have you ever been terribly alone,
— even when other people were all around you?

Perhaps you were walking down a street,
totally absorbed in some personal crisis,
and, despite people coming and going beside you
it seemed there was no one to whom you could go
for encouragement and counsel.

The business of decision-making
is often a lonely matter.

Sometimes you lie awake at night,
when everyone else has gone to sleep.

And you go over in your mind
the worries and decisions of the day past
and of the one to come.

Late one evening
in the last week of his life,
Jesus and the disciples were walking together.

They were climbing a hill in the darkness.
Eventually they came to an olive orchard.

More precisely to a place
where olives are crushed for their oil.

When they came to the edge of the orchard
Jesus asked the disciples to remain there
while he spent some time in prayer.

Then he took three of them,
the inner three, Peter, James and John,
and together the four men went farther on
up the side of the hill a little way.

The inner three were special friends.
Peter had sworn an oath never to deny his master,
no matter who else did,
no matter what should happen as a result of it.

James and John had made a bold claim
that they were prepared to share with Jesus
whatever might happen to him anywhere.

The three men, Peter, James and John,
were the obvious men to be with Jesus
when he most needed the support of close friends.

He shared with them something of his terrible burden.
He told them that what was on his mind
was an issue so serious, so all-consuming, so worrisome,
that he would as soon be dead as deal with it.

In fact, death would be preferable to life
unless he found some relief from his anxiety.

And all he asked of his three friends
was their watchful presence with him.

He needed to know that they were nearby
while he struggled with his lonely decision-making.

The way before him seemed an obvious one,
— and it was certain to lead to his death.

And so he prayed that some other way
might be found acceptable for him to take.

The depth of his desolation found words
in his plea for relief from his responsibility.

Yet hardly had his prayer been spoken
when he turned to God in obedience and trust.

"Not what I would like to do," he said
"but what you would have me do!"

Decision-making is a lonely business.
And the more serious the decision,
the lonelier it is in making it.

In the midst of his tormented indecision
he turned, naturally enough,
to his friends for support.

And they were sound asleep!
They were indifferent
to what was happening to him.

And seemingly unaware
of what was required of them.

And because they slept during the time of crisis,
they were disobedient to their brave promises.

Promises both of loyalty and of participation
in whatever might happen to him.

Each of three times Jesus came to his disciples
for support and encouragement.

And each of three times the disciples slept on.

The gospel of Mark
was written for a congregation
in which men and women were being harassed
by people hostile to the new faith.

The temptation in the church was to give in
during these times of crucial decision-making,
and to come to terms with the world.

In that way a Christian could escape persecution,
and perhaps even death as well.

In this account of Jesus in the garden
the church was shown how he prepared
for his hearings and trials
before those who were hostile to him.

He prepared for his later rejection
and humiliating experiences of all sorts
through prayer to the One he called Father.

As a result of his time with God in prayer
he faced the future in obedience and trust.

The Christian way to resist whatever opposes you,
according to Mark, is to be prayerful and vigilant.

The instruction to "watch and pray"
given to the disciples in the Garden of Gethsemane
is an instruction to Christians everywhere and always.

These same words of Jesus
come with fresh urgency to the church today.

They are an appeal to disciples everywhere
to be aware of what is happening all around us.

And a call to recognize as our source of strength
a life of prayer.

This means, surely, that in our day
the greatest responsibility rests on those of us
who belong to his band of disciples.

You are like James and John, and I am like Peter
in that we have given publicly lifetime
pledges of loyalty and commitment to Christ.

He has found us sleeping,
when we ought to have been watchful and careful
of all the distractions on our loyalty to him.

He has found us sleeping,
and without a word in our defense,
when we ought to have been at prayer
for the strength we need to meet the crises
of faith and practice that confront us each day.

And we haven't been at prayer
because it is at once the most obvious
and the most difficult thing in the world to do.

―――――――――

Jesus was isolated by the disciples.
He was left alone when he needed them most,
so that as companions they might face
a history-making crossroad together.

However, at the crossroad
the disciples had already begun
to look in one direction and Jesus in the other.

The misunderstanding of Jesus by his followers
in the olive orchard outside Jerusalem
was not a matter of harmless naivety.

It was then a matter of life and death,
— for them as well as for him.

                                    — Amen.

Prayer

Mark 14:32-42

Mighty God, we remember Gethsemane.
We remember the prayer of Jesus
— in his sorrow and in his despair.

We remember his loneliness in the Garden,
— in his need for human companionship,
understanding and support.

We remember the sleep of the disciples,
— in their misunderstanding both of Jesus
and of themselves.

Help us, Mighty God,
to prepare for the crises in our lives,
to prepare for the challenges to our faith,
as did Jesus,
by the practice of prayer,
and the discipline of watchfulness.
In Jesus' name.
Amen.

Jesus — Betrayed And Arrested

The Bitterness Of Betrayal

2
Jesus — Betrayed And Arrested
"The Bitterness Of Betrayal"

Psalm 55:13-15   **Mark 14:43-50**

When he was an old man
he wanted to speak to a friend
about certain people whose offenses
he had never forgiven.

He had been the unwanted child,
so he had been told,
of an elderly father and a young mother.

He had been born into a home
that was exceedingly religious
in a narrow strict and hard way.

It was a home
in which there was more law than gospel,
certainly more law than love.

As the little boy grew up,
the influence of his father faded away.

And he was brought up
by his young mother and an uncle.

The uncle became his idol.
He imitated his uncle in every possible way.

The uncle was his friend.
It was to his uncle he ran
when he was hurt or frightened
or when he had a secret to share.

No little boy ever loved an uncle
as he came to love this wonderful man.

One day, a Sunday,
he started off as usual for Sunday school.

Along the road
he met some other little boys his own age.

Together they spent a happy morning,
running, laughing and playing ball.

They forgot all about church,
Sunday school or anything else.

When lunchtime came
they all went back to their homes.

With a great shock,
he realized that his mother and aunts
were really furious with him.

He managed to avoid getting caught,
because he was little and quick,
and so ran outdoors and down the road again.

After they had eaten the noon meal
his mother and her sisters came looking for him.

He avoided them all,
but with increasing difficulty and mounting fear.

And then, his beloved uncle appeared!
And all at once his terror disappeared.

The sight of his uncle meant that
he would receive mercy,
understanding and a fair hearing.

And perhaps a light punishment as well,
which by this time he believed he must deserve.

His uncle called to him:
"Come, Leslie, come to me. No one will hurt you."

And with great a shudder of relief
he ran straight into the arms of the one person
he loved and trusted more than anyone else.

His uncle held him tightly.
He delivered him at once to his mother.

With the help of her sisters
his mother gave her little boy a terrible beating,
a truly terrible beating.

As an old man, he still remembered the pain.
He could still feel the blows raining on his body.

And worse by far than the pain
was the memory of his betrayal by his uncle.

The sad deep hurt in his eyes
as he told the story many years later,
was not alone the memory of physical abuse.

It was rather the memory of a deep trust
and a tender love that had been betrayed.

To be betrayed by anyone is a dreadful experience.
To be betrayed by a friend or a loved one
is the cruelest betrayal of all.

———————

While he and his disciples were in the Garden,
Jesus had been betrayed several times.
He had gone there with 11 disciples to pray.

And he had asked only that they should stay with him,
— watchful and supportive.

These were men who had voluntarily given him
such oaths of loyalty
as any leader might thrill to hear:
"If necessary I will die with you,
but I will never deny you."

And it was not only Peter, James and John
who said these things.
So did the other men as well.

Their brave words were in marked contrast
to their weak actions which came later.

While Jesus was resigning himself to the inevitable,
which meant his death, his disciples slept on,
totally indifferent to it all.

———————

His betrayal by the disciples closest to him
was followed by the betrayal of the disciple
who, earlier in the evening, had gone his own way.

And then, with an armed arresting party
Judas arrived quietly in the dark garden.

There was no warning of their arrival.
The disciples who had been left on watch
were fast asleep.

Judas came into the garden in the guise of a disciple.
And with the greeting of a disciple
he marked out his Master for the arrest.

He was seized.
There was a scuffle.
And one person was wounded.

In his remarks to those who arrested him
Jesus exposed their misunderstanding both
of who he was and of their own cowardice.

"Have you come out as against a robber," he asked,
"armed as if to arrest a dangerous criminal?"

"I was with you every day in the temple preaching,
and you made no attempt to arrest me."

Despite the protection of numbers,
they had lacked the courage to arrest Jesus
by daylight in the temple.

Their bravery after dark with a paid guide
was an empty cowardly charade.

He was arrested by his own people.
Just as he had been betrayed by his closest friends.

The bitterness of betrayal
was a significant part of his passion.

In fact, some teachers have suggested
that what took place in the orchard at night
was more painful than all that took place
before noon the next day!

There was a tremendous lot behind the text which reads:
"They all forsook him and fled."

Mark wanted his readers to appreciate
that just as Jesus had been betrayed by Judas
so he had been betrayed by all the other disciples as well.

He wanted his readers to feel for themselves
the consequences of brave pledges of loyalty,
when there is nothing with which to back them up.

And in this account of the arrest of Jesus
Mark warned his readers against a confession of faith
that comes too easily.

Too easily that is,
unless they understood the consequences
of what it was they were claiming to be.

In the midst of their common sufferings
he wanted them to see
that even within the first circle of disciples
there was betrayal and defection in the face of danger.

When Jesus is betrayed
it is always his followers who do it.

No one else can betray him,
because no one else has ever given him
a pledge of their love and loyalty.

Sometimes he is betrayed in the quiet of our hearts,
when our love for him dies for lack of loving.

Sometimes he is betrayed when one is too frightened
to stand for what is Christian,
or to stand against what is dehumanizing in the world.

If eventually the first disciples
achieved positions of prestige in the church,
it was not because they had been brave, courageous or loyal
when these qualities were most needed.

If eventually these people lived worthy lives
it is because sometimes God is able to work wonders
— even with those who have betrayed his Son.

— Amen.

Prayer

Mark 14:43-50

Mighty God,
we remember the betrayals of Jesus in the Garden.
We remember the slumbers of those
who had professed loyalty and support
if need be, to death itself.

We remember the betrayal of Judas
under the sign of obedient discipleship.
We remember the arrest of Jesus,
accompanied by violence and bloodshed.

We remember the desertion of every disciple,
so that Jesus was left alone
in the hands of his enemies.

Lord Jesus,
to whom the bitterness of betrayal
and the loneliness of desertion
came from the hands of your disciples,
help us in our living neither to betray you,
nor to desert you, the Lord of our lives.
— Amen.

Jesus Before The High Priest

The Loneliness of Injustice

3
Jesus Before The High Priest
"The Loneliness Of Injustice"

Psalm 26   **Mark 14:53-65**

Some of the persons
who heard Jesus teaching in the temple,
but who misunderstood what it was he had to say,
were produced at his church trial.

They had misunderstood Jesus so badly
that they were unable to agree amongst themselves
on what it was he had said.

They had heard him say something
about the temple and its destruction.

And therefore, they assumed
that he had threatened to destroy it.

And further,
that he had intended to replace it
with one "not made with hands."

Mark says that these people were false witnesses.
These were people to whom the truth
would have been a stranger.

They never intended to tell the truth.
They were interested only
in co-operating for a conviction.

Their stories didn't agree with one another.
As a result of which their evidence was useless,
and ought to have been thrown out of court.

An attempt was made to have Jesus reply
to the false trumped-up charges against him.

He remained silent.
He refused to refute lies either about his person
or about his teaching.

A little later he was asked
whether he was the Messiah,
the Christ, the Son of God.

This was a different matter entirely,
and Jesus answered it affirmatively.

"I am the Messiah,
I am the Christ; the one who fulfills
the prophecies of the Old Testament,
and the hopes of all those
who look for the end of all things."

The representatives of true religion
reacted to this admission on his part as people do
who are scandalized beyond belief.

"Blasphemy!" they cried,
and not for the first time.

They had chanted the same thing against him,
at the beginning of his ministry,
when he had pardoned the sins of a paralyzed man.

He had done then, according to them,
what otherwise only God can do.

He was claiming now what no person had the right to claim,
— a special place in relation to God.

Jesus was not yet condemned to death,
— the court seems not to have had that authority.

And so it condemned him as deserving death.
They needed only the means of inflicting the death penalty.

In the meantime,
they began to treat him as if his death
had already been decided.

When confronted with the tales of false witnesses,
Jesus remained silent.

When asked to identify himself in terms of the truth,
he spoke without hesitation.

In the end, therefore,
he was condemned for telling the truth.

And once again, as earlier in the olive orchard,
Jesus was alone.

His own received him not!
He was condemned as deserving death
— without a dissenting voice.

As a result, the process of rejection was complete.
The whole nation, as represented by the Council,
had rejected its Messiah sent from God.

In the years that followed his condemnation,
one of the questions that bothered the early Christians
had to do with the messiahship of Jesus.

How was it possible for the Messiah
to have been rejected, condemned and crucified?

This passage from Mark's gospel answers that question.
It was possible because his teaching was misunderstood.

And he was condemned as deserving death, as worthy of death,
for telling the truth about himself.

He was crucified, according to Mark,
by his own people who knew precisely what they were doing.

And no one had intervened to support him.
His friends behaved like enemies.

And when that happened there was no possibility
his death could have been prevented.

All the way through the beautiful gospel of Mark
there is a contrast between who Jesus actually is,
and the way in which he is treated.

The One for whom his people prayed and waited
was humiliated, rejected and left alone when he came.

———————

There has never been a time
when the church did not need to hear this story.

It comes to us,
as it came to its first readers and hearers,
with the example of Jesus.

When he was slandered, he said nothing.
And always he was ready to tell the truth,
regardless of the consequences.

This story comes to us, as it came to the early church,
with a clear confessional statement about Jesus.

He is the Christ of God!
He is the fulfillment of the Old Testament prophecies.
He is at the right hand of God.
He will act as judge in the reign of God among us.
He shares in the power and the glory of God.

These are the statements,
and these are the truths
to which the Christians in Rome
were told to hold fast.

And what was true for them,
is true as well for us.

— Amen.

Prayer

Mark 14:53-65

Mighty God,
we think of all the bad things
that happen to good people.

We think about the injustice in our society;
of the lies told about innocent people,
of the ways in which people are manipulated
and used against their will,
of the inhumanity in our established institutions.

We remember these things too
were the experiences of Jesus.

We remember his silence
in the face of falsehoods about his teaching.

We remember his courage
in the challenge to his identity.

We remember his loneliness
in his rejection by those he came to save.

Help us, Good Lord,
so to confess Jesus as the Lord of all life
that by our words and deeds we challenge injustice
in his name, wherever it appears.
— Amen.

The Denial
By Peter

The Scandal
Of Disloyalty

4
The Denial By Peter
"The Scandal Of Disloyalty"

Psalm 62   **Mark 14:53-54; 66-72**

This is the last scene in which Peter is involved.
As often happens throughout the gospel of Mark
Peter is the representative disciple.

He represents the other 10, maybe the whole 12.
Until this time the other disciples
were as much to blame as he was
in their betrayals of Jesus.

He had taken an oath, voluntarily,
to stay with Jesus until death, if necessary.

The others had said the same thing.
The betrayal, when it came in the orchard,
involved all of the disciples.

"They all forsook him and fled."
As the story is told in this passage
there is hope that the senior disciple
will redeem himself in terms of loyalty, courage,
commitment and faithfulness.

We cannot really believe
that we have seen him at his best

when he was found in embarrassed sleep,
— while his master was praying for his life.

The text says that Peter followed Jesus
"at a distance," which seems not a bad way
to describe his discipleship until now.

And even at that, he might have stayed where he was
except that without warning temptation appeared again.

It appeared this time in the form of a servant girl,
who would have known little or nothing of Jesus.

Certainly she would not have known or understood
why he was undergoing a hearing in her master's house.

The girl thought she recognized Peter from some place.
It was saucy of her to say so, but she commented in passing
that she had seen Peter with Jesus:
— it might have been at the fish market or in the temple area.

It was Peter's turn to be somewhat confused.
He thought he was being accused of being a follower of Jesus.

Actually, at that moment, he was linked with Jesus
only by a physical association of some sort.

In his embarrassment, confusion and irritation he said:
"I neither know nor understand what you mean."

And for that moment, in spite of himself,
Peter was caught in a moment of truth.

It is certain he does not know who Jesus is,
nor what it means to be "with him" as a follower.

Much less does he understand
the meaning of the relationship between them.

He misunderstood the maiden as well.
He thinks she means one thing, discipleship,
when she was interested only in his association with Jesus.

Peter didn't intend to make such a clumsy answer.
Or to tell such a silly lie, but he did both just the same.

The servant girl didn't give up easily.
It was good fun to tease the big uneasy man,
and it drew remarkable attention to herself.

In order to avoid further attention
Peter retreated to a quiet corner by himself.

Now there had doubtless been some conversation
amongst the bystanders following the remark by the girl
and the abrupt denial by Peter.

Even those who didn't like her impudent manner
were interested in the truth of what she had said.

The man from Nazareth, now upstairs with the High Priest,
had been a Rabbi of sorts and he did have followers.
A dozen or more.

They were such nondescript characters
that people didn't particularly remember
what they looked like or who they were.

Pointing now to a humiliated and possibly angry Peter
the tiresome girl said again: "This man is one of them."

Once again Peter denied any association at all with Jesus.
He didn't know the man at all.

He had simply come in from the street
for a place at the fire
and a bit of whatever gossip was on the go.

That might have worked, had not his accent betrayed him.
He was a man from Galilee with a Galilean accent.
He had a soft "r" and a hard "g" sound in his speech.

How terribly unfair
when, despite every effort to the contrary,
one cannot shed his/her national or local origins.

To be identified solely by the give away in one's accent
is rarely helpful or complimentary.

By this time the bystanders had heard him speak.
They might have been slow enough in other ways,
but not so slow that they were mistaken about Peter.

He was a Galilean!

And they said so, after a while,
to the big man who was alone in the dark,
— with only his conscience for company.

And his conscience was poor company that evening.
This time Peter denied everything,
— his homeland in the north of the country,
and his relationship with Jesus as well.

He swore an oath to that effect:
"So help me God, let me be struck dead if I lie,
but I do not know this man of whom you speak."

———————

In the Garden of Gethsemane
three times Jesus had come to Peter for support.

And three times Peter had been sound asleep.
After each time Jesus had been left
to face alone his confrontation with God.

In the courtyard of the High Priest
temptation had come three times to Peter
in the guise of a servant girl and some onlookers.
And three times Peter had given in to it.
Three times he denied, the last time with an oath,
any relationship whatever with Jesus.

This was the final rejection of Jesus by the disciples.
The desertion of Jesus by the disciples was now complete.

In this scene Jesus was denied for the last time
by those who knew him best and whom he loved most.

There was nothing left in their relationship to betray.
In the person of Peter, they had done it all.

And somewhere, in the distance, for the second time,
came the crowing sound of a rooster.

The only person who really heard it that morning
went to pieces and wept like a child.

This final betrayal by his followers
is more frightful even than that of Judas.

It is a moving, tragic story.

The story of Peter reminded the church
of the way in which Jesus
dealt with the questions put to him.

It reminded the church of the contrast between Jesus
and the manner in which Peter handled the comments
from the servant girl.

Comments in the first instance he completely misunderstood.
By the time Mark had written his gospel
many members of the church had been on trial.

Many of them had been on trial before judges
who were convinced in advance of their guilt as Christians.

With the real possibility before them
of their children left fatherless and motherless
they too, like Peter, had compromised their faith.

The story of Peter, offensive as it was,
was an encouragement to all of them.

If he could deny Jesus as he had done,
and betray his trust, as he had done,
and yet display heroic characteristics later,
so might they!

Although his shameful behavior was known far and wide,
it was also known, with gratitude, that he had,
in the end witnessed a good confession in Christ
and given his life for it.

The lesser-known Christians, wherever they were,
with the example of Peter before them,
might not despair when they gave way under interrogation
or threat of pain and death.

They too might live in hope.

The story of Peter taught the church
that the time to fight any temptation to deny Christ
is long before the crisis comes.

The shameful scene that had taken place
in the courtyard of the High Priest
had been decided long before.

The battle with the temptation to deny Christ
had been lost long before it was fought.

According to Mark,
Jesus had warned Peter,
and the warning comes as much to us as it did to him,
to "watch and pray that you do not give in
during the time of temptation."

The story of Peter in the courtyard
reminded the church ever afterward
that without the Spirit of God in his life
even the Chief of the Apostles was a failure.

The story reminded the church
that ultimately there can be no foundation for it
other than Jesus Christ her Lord.

It makes no difference where we are, or who we are,
we must confess our faith in Jesus as Lord
whenever the opportunity presents itself
or the situation demands it.

— Amen.

Prayer

Mark 14:53-54; 66-72

Mighty God,
we have listened to the scandal
of a disciple denying his Lord.

We have heard him protest his ignorance
of what it means to be with Jesus.

We have heard him deny any association
with the One in whose steps he followed.

We have heard his frightful curse
as he denied the Man from Galilee.

We too, Holy Father,
have warmed ourselves at the fires of the world.

We too have felt the temptation to deny our Lord.
And we fear to feel it again.

Give us such knowledge of him,
and such depth of loyalty to him,
that we may not ever deny him.
In his name.
Amen.

Jesus Brought Before Imperial Rome

The Dignity Of Silence

5

Jesus Brought Before Imperial Rome
"The Dignity Of Silence"

Isaiah 43:1-13   **Mark 15:1-5**

It was early in the morning.
The representatives of the Jewish people
held an important meeting.

They met to compose a charge on which
they could have Jesus brought before the military governor.

The military governor was a senior civil servant from Rome.
He was called a procurator.
In this case he was a hard man.

He ruled by decree, a cruel decree if necessary,
without consideration for the feelings of the local people.

One Jewish historian has written that this man
had been guilty of rape, insult, murder and inhumanity.

Later on, when he had carried cruelty too far,
he was recalled from Judea and replaced by another man.

When Jesus was brought before him,
Pilate was at the peak of his power and influence.

It is unlikely he had ever seen Jesus before.
He may not even have heard of him
until a few hours before their first and last meeting.

In the gospel story we have only a digest
of what took place at the meeting of Pilate with Jesus.

On that point everyone agrees.
The gospel itself suggests it.

The main charge against Jesus
was that he had claimed to be "The King of the Jews."

This is the first time any mention is made of Jesus as a King.
And there is a good reason for that.

As a Roman Governor, Pilate would have had no interest at all
in a religious charge of blasphemy.

What possible difference could it have made to him
whether Jesus claimed to be the Messiah or the Son of God?

He would have turned on his heel in contempt
of any such religious quarrel as beneath his concern.

And so the authorities laid a charge
in terms Pilate had not been able to ignore.

Anyone claiming to be a King, the King of the Jews,
represented a threat to the Roman Governor
and the whole military establishment in Judea.

A pretender to the throne in Judea was guilty of treason.
And those who followed such a person
would be guilty of rebellion against Roman authority.

The punishment for both charges was death.
And so it was that Pilate,
who seemed totally indifferent to Jesus as a person,
dealt first with the major charge of treason.

"Do you claim to be the King of the Jews?" he asked.
And the answer from Jesus was a vague one.

It was not an admission. It was not a denial either.
"You have said so," he replied.

There is here the possibility that Jesus was/is a King,
— although not in the sense that concerned Pilate.

And not in the sense his accusers hoped to suggest.
After the main charge had been laid,
there were many other accusations laid against Jesus
by the religious authorities.

In this gospel we are not told what they were.
Whether true or false, they must have represented
some sort of challenge to the political set-up of the day.

Otherwise Pilate would not have listened to them.
Sometimes, in its eagerness to secure a verdict,
the prosecution will overstate its case against the accused.

Sometimes an attempt is made, if only by suggestion,
to construct a stronger case than the evidence will bear.

Whether this was true when Jesus appeared before Pilate
we will never know.

We do know that Pilate began to wonder
whether all he was hearing was correct.

Especially in view of the silence of the accused.
The silence of Jesus is the most dignified response he could
     make,
in the face of the persistent interrogation by his enemies,
and in view of the sly attempt to destroy him by innuendo.

And all of it against the background of a mob
so stirred up that it clamored for his death.

The rejection of Jesus,
begun in the first scene of the passion story,
reached another level in this passage.

He who had been rejected by his friends,
his disciples and his religious leaders,
is here rejected by the people of Jerusalem.

The figure of the Man from Nazareth,
alone now in spirit as well as in body,
rejected by everyone with whom he had come in contact
during the last week of his life,
is a picture we shall not soon forget.

Sometimes the truth is told when people least intend it to be so.
It had happened with Peter
when he denied any knowledge of Jesus
as he shifted uneasily in the courtyard of the High Priest.

It happened again in the charge against Jesus before Pilate.
He stood charged with being "The King of the Jews."
Or of claiming to be "The King of the Jews."

And anyone claiming to be a King,
who was not in political obedience to Rome,
was a threat to be dealt with quickly and finally.

Jesus was not that kind of King.
And yet the gospel understands him to be no less a King
for all that.

The Man who stood, hands bound behind his back,
was and is indeed "The King of the Jews."

His authority was and is one of love,
and it is exercised as an act of love.

His power lies in his defenselessness.
His glory was demonstrated in his suffering and death
on behalf of Jews and non-Jews alike worldwide.

He is the Lord of all,
but it is a lordship he has never imposed on anyone.

Except for the company of two thieves,
he died alone, rejected and misunderstood
by those on whose behalf he was put to death.

This gospel passage reminds us
that right from the beginning there were disciples
who abandoned Jesus under pressures of all sorts.
Leaving him alone.

There were leaders in the church, as in the synagogue,
who from the outset denied a commitment to Jesus.
Leaving him alone.

These verses remind us
that those who welcomed him to their city
soon rejected him and "the ways of God."

They chose in his place
someone who symbolized violence and terrorism.
Leaving him alone.

And just as it happened "once upon a time,"
so it has happened throughout Christian history
wherever Christian communities were established.

And it happens now wherever he is "King" in name only.
Leaving him alone.

— Amen.

Prayer

Mark 15:1-5

Mighty God,
help us to know the good meaning of silence.
And how it may refresh our lives.
Help us to experience the healing of silence.
And how it may mend our minds and bodies.
Help us to appreciate the power of silence.
And how it may bring love into our lives.
Help us to know the strength of silence.
And how it may speak against evil in the world.

Defend us from the cowardice of silence,
when we ought to speak out and don't.
Protect us from the hurt and harm of silence,
whenever it is used against us.
In this silence ... hear us.
— Amen.

The Crucifixion

The Rejection Of Royalty

6

The Crucifixion
"The Rejection Of Royalty"

Psalm 22:1-21   **Mark 15:21-32**

The language in this passage is remarkably restrained.
There is no attempt in it to create sympathy for Jesus.

There is no attempt to incite hatred toward those
responsible for the actual crucifixion itself.

This is an event far too solemn for that sort of thing.
The facts are stated and left to stand for themselves.
There is no additional comment of any kind.

In a passage where the language is so carefully chosen
the reader must go through it slowly and thoughtfully.

Otherwise we might miss what is being said.
The enemies of Jesus believed they had destroyed him.
They believed that they had seen the end of him.

And yet, nothing happened, according to Mark,
that should have surprised anyone who knew his/her Bible.

For all unknown alike to the friends and enemies of Jesus
in some mysterious way, the things they did and said
had always been a part of the eternal plan of God.

It is a great mystery, certainly, but one the church believes,
that in the events surrounding the death of Jesus,
the purposes of God were being fulfilled.

He was put to death — with criminals.
He was offered a drink of wine that had been drugged.
His clothing became the prizes in a lottery.

And while he hung on the cross
he was mocked and humiliated by those who passed him by.

All these things about the Messiah, the Servant of God,
a careful reader might have found in certain psalms[1]
and in the book of Isaiah.

And it is from the perspective of those writings
that Mark composed his gospel.

They were proof, surely, all evidence to the contrary,
that the will of God was being fulfilled
as it had been predicted in the Hebrew Bible.

As a part of the pre-crucifixion routine
Jesus had been brutally beaten.

It was a procedure that brought men to the edge of death.
And sometimes to death itself.

It is quite likely he needed help to carry the cross-beam
of his cross as the procession left the city for Golgotha.

The man chosen to help him was called Simon, a native of
Cyrene.

He must carry the cross-beam in the place of another man,
— Simon Peter of Galilee.

We hardly need a reminder at this point
that Simon Peter had pledged himself to die with Jesus,
if that should have been necessary.[2]

Instead of denying himself,[3]
taking up the cross and following after his master,
he denied his master.

And so another man, another Simon,
must do under orders what Peter had offered to do voluntarily.

By the time the gospel was written,
Peter had in fact been martyred in Rome.
And doubtless in that situation
he had carried his cross in every sense of the word.

But on the day of the crucifixion of Jesus,
when the disciple from Galilee ought to have done it,
it was a native of Cyprus who carried the cross-beam.

The contrast between the pledges of a disciple
and his actual performance in a time of crisis
does not end with Peter.

Earlier in the gospel[4], two of the disciples,
James and John, asked for the chief places with Jesus
when he came into his glory.

They asked that when the great day came
they might be one at his right hand and one at his left.

At the time of their request Jesus had warned them:
"You don't know what you are asking."

And neither they did!
When his royalty was demonstrated on the cross
Jesus had other companions with him.

In the places of James and John, his disciples,
he had the fellowship of two robbers.

They were one on his right and the other one on his left.
Just as Peter ought to have been carrying the cross,
so the ambitious brothers ought to have been with him then.

However, they had dreams of more comfortable places.
They had dreams of a cup brimming over with the good life,
and of a baptism into a different sort of society altogether.

It is true, though, that, like Peter,
they were to follow Jesus later.

In the meantime, the chief places on either side of him
were taken by two men from the city jail.

Men who were crucified were put to death
where they could be seen by the largest number of people.

Their deaths were a warning to all who saw them
that imperial power did not deal lightly
with those who dared oppose it.

Jesus was put to death in a place called Golgotha,
— so named because it was shaped like a human skull.

There is an old Jewish legend
that the skull of Adam was buried at Golgotha.

"If through Adam disobedience, sin and death came into
    the world,"
wrote Paul, "through Jesus there is obedience and life to undo
    Adam's wrong."[5]
The connection of Golgotha with both Adam and Jesus
is one that Mark would have us make.

People who were crucified were put to death
in a location at eye-level with the traffic that passed by.

The body of the victim was bent in an "S" shape
to keep its feet from touching the ground.

53

As he hung dying, the criminal was frequently subjected
to the taunts and tortures of heartless folk
who saw him there completely helpless.

In his dying, Jesus was despised and rejected by passers-by,
by religious leaders and authorities,
and by those who were put to death with him.

The reactions of those who watched him die
served only to underline the complete abandonment of Jesus.

It was a procedure that had begun long before.
The passers-by were right and wrong
in the things they said and did to Jesus.

"You who would destroy the temple and build it in three days,
save yourself and come down from the cross."[6]

They were unable to know it then,
that in his death he was destroying all that temple worship
had stood for in its sacrificial system.

And in his dying he was replacing it with another way to God,
himself, to be raised from the dead in three days.

The religious leaders, for their part, also had sport with him.
They called out "He saved others, himself he cannot save."
And that was precisely true!

He had saved others, from their sins and diseases.
Yet finally, in order to do as much for us,
he could not and would not save himself.

We believe in him today
precisely because he did not come down from the cross,
precisely because he did not turn back from the plan of God,
as he was challenged to do.

And then the men on either side of him
joined the passing parade of pathetic people
in their outpouring of contempt and hostility toward him.

In fact, according to the text of Mark,
what they said was not fit even to be recorded.

The rejection and abandonment of Jesus,
even the horror of crucifixion itself,
have been the experiences of more people
than we will ever know.

It happens, in one form or other,
as often in our village, town or city
as it does in any other part of the world.

And while that is true, and we know it is,
what happened on Golgotha was different in nature.

What happened there was a part of the plan of God
for your salvation and for mine.

— Amen.

---

[1]Psalms 22 and 69
[2]Mark 14:31
[3]Mark 8:27f
[4]Mark 10:37, 40
[5]Romans 5:19
[6]Mark 15:29, 30

Prayer

Mark 15:21-32

Mighty God,
the God of our Lord Jesus Christ,
gather us up in the great company
of those to whom salvation has come
through the cross of Christ.

Let the redeeming power of his love
flow through us and transform us
as it has done for generations before us.

Kneeling before you,
let us find forgiveness, wholeness and peace.

Here let us determine from this time forward
to share with Christ the burden of suffering
wherever we meet it in the world.

Here let us begin all over again
to live, work, speak and pray
as those whose lives have been given back to them,
through the death of Christ our Savior.
— Amen.

The Final
Abandonment

Who Was
The One
Who Died?

7

The Final Abandonment
"Who Was The One Who Died?"

Psalm 31:9-24

Mark 15:33-39

On Thursday evening, in the darkness of an olive orchard
Jesus had asked for the support of his disciples.

In particular, he had asked for the support
of Peter, James and John while he went a little distance away.

He went off to pray for relief from the necessity
to drink from the cup of suffering he could see before him.

They seemed to do as he had asked them,
when in fact they were indifferent to his request.

They were tired from the events of the day,
and so they took the opportunity to have a sleep.

This meant, of course, that he was left to agonize alone.
And while his closest friends were sleeping,
his enemies were wide awake and were on the move.

During that same evening, in the darkness,
possibly near midnight, he was arrested by an armed mob.

His disciples, all of whom, including the inner three,
had sworn loyalty to him until death if need be,
fled for their lives from the armed mob.
And he was left alone.

In the courtyard of the High Priest,
while he was being questioned,
his senior disciple denied all knowledge of him.

He was physically deserted by the only disciple
who had followed him that far.

Jesus was left to face an unknown future alone.
Later on, the religious leaders of his own people
accused him before a Roman official they all hated.

While charges that were inconsistent with one another
were shouted back and forth around him,
he maintained a dignified silence.

Condemned to death by a man who feared public pressure,
he was beaten so badly he needed help to carry his cross-beam.

A stranger carried it,
and two strangers were put to death with him.

The gospel of Mark at this point
has provided us with a poignant picture of Jesus;
— betrayed by a man he had called and trusted,
— deserted by all the rest of his disciples,
— falsely accused by his own people,
and ridiculed by complete strangers.

And now as it was in the Garden of Gethsemane,
once again he was in darkness.

The darkness this time is not the sort that follows sunset.
It was rather the sort of darkness
that accompanied great events in ancient history.

When he speaks of "darkness at noon"
Mark is telling his readers that the death of Jesus
was an event that affected the whole universe.

What was done on Golgotha, he is saying,
was of ultimate significance for any place in the world,
and for every place in the world at any time.

Our spiritual ancestors understood the darkness at noonday
as a reflection as well of the dark night of the soul
through which Jesus had been passing.

When it was over, he cried out to God
in words that have been remembered ever since.[1]

They came, we believe, as the climax to his experience
of being betrayed, deserted and abandoned by humankind.

"My God, My God, why has Thou forsaken me?"
This is the final abandonment!

At this point Jesus was totally deserted and completely alone!
The cup of suffering had been drained even to the dregs.

The loneliness of Jesus' suffering
is a loneliness his people have always known.

Pain brings with it a particular loneliness.
It cannot be shared, not really.
It must be borne alone.

The absence of God is an experience that means something
only to those who have ever known the presence of God.

And the presence of God is still a reality,
if, in the midst of feeling completely forsaken,
we are able to cry out "My God."

It is the experience of countless believers
that, when all our resources have been exhausted
and every experience denies the presence of God,
the strength is still provided to search for God.

The presence of God is real at all times,
and in terrible places.

Even when we cannot bear to think of God at all,
or even if we are able only to rail at God and against God,
that is precisely what the psalmist tells us to do.

In a strange sort of way Jesus was misunderstood to the end.
Even the words of his final appeal to God
were misunderstood by those who heard them.

Some people thought he was calling for Elijah.
Out of curiosity to see whether Elijah
would come to rescue this Son of Israel at the last moment,
they tried to keep him alive.

Then, writes Mark, Jesus died "with a loud cry."
He died violently.

As a result of his death,
and more precisely as a result of what followed his death,
the religious life of humankind was forever transformed.

No longer was it a way of salvation for a few,
whether by right of office, race or religion.

The church has taught ever since
that by his death and resurrection,
the gates of the kingdom of God
were thrown open to all believers.

The final hour, the end of time, all is over.
And you and I are making our way,
however slowly and painfully,
toward the wonderful God who loves us all.

Who then was the One who died?
Who was the One who died
as a result of the treachery of Judas,
as a consequence of the betrayal of the disciples,
as a sequel to the denial by Peter,
as a result of the conspiracy of his own people?

He was a Jewish son of Galilee.
He was a son of Mary,
whose name has ever since been immortalized.

He was a teacher of great charisma,
a healer known for his compassion,
a young prophet, a true spokesman for God.

And we believe he was more even than all of those things.
He was, whatever else, the Son of God.

And through him God has made the right of everyone
the gifts of healing, wholeness and peace.

Through him God has given us
the priceless gift of salvation.

— Amen.

---

[1]Much has been written on these words, variously called "The Cry of Dereliction," "The Cry of Despair, "The Shout of Victory." One of the most lengthy and thoughtful works is a relatively new one by Lorraine Caza, called *Mon Dieu, Porquoi M'As tu Abandonne?*, published by Les Editions Belarmin, Montreal, 1989.

Prayer

Mark 15:33-39

Good and gracious God,
to whom our personal stories are known,
and by whom we are loved and loved again,
you know our feelings of loneliness for your presence.

In all our dark times
help us to know your presence all about us,
to forgive us, to heal us, to restore us to you.

Help us
to deal with misunderstanding, rejection,
lies and betrayal as did Jesus.

Help us
to deal with those who would impose
their greed, their hunger for power, their envy
on us or on those whose love sustains us.

Help us
to see in the One crucified for us,
and raised by you to glory,
the Lord and Savior of the world.
— Amen.

Appendix

A Suggested Outline
For A Three-Hour Liturgy
On
The Passion According To St. Mark

Music for meditation while the people gather

Silent Prayer

Sentences And Responses

1. Jesus In Gethsemane

Hymn: "Go To Dark Gethsemane"

Scriptures: Psalm 43; Mark 14:32-42

Meditation: "Jesus — Misunderstood And Alone"

Prayer And Silence

2. Jesus — Betrayed And Arrested

Hymn: "Man Of Sorrows, Wondrous Name"

Scriptures: Psalm 55:13-15; Mark 14:43-50

Meditation: "The Bitterness Of Betrayal"

Prayer And Silence

3. Jesus Before The High Priest

Hymn: "Ah, Holy Jesus, How Hast Thou Offended?"

Scriptures: Psalm 26; Mark 14:53-65

Meditation: "The Loneliness Of Injustice"

Prayer And Silence

4. The Denial By Peter

Hymn: "There Is A Green Hill Far Away"

Scriptures: Psalm 62; Mark 14:53-54; 66-72

Meditation: "The Scandal Of Disloyalty"

Prayer And Silence

5. Jesus Brought Before Imperial Rome

Hymn: "When I Survey The Wondrous Cross"

Scriptures: Isaiah 43:1-13; Mark 15:1-5

Meditation: "The Dignity Of Silence"

Prayer And Silence

6. The Crucifixion

Hymn: "Were You There?"

Scriptures: Psalm 22:1-21; Mark 15:21-32

Meditation: "The Rejection Of Royalty"

Prayer And Silence

7. The Final Abandonment

Hymn: "O Sacred Head, Sore Wounded"

Scriptures: Psalm 31:9-24; Mark 15:33-39

Meditation: "Who Was The One Who Died?"

Prayer And Silence

Hymn: "The King Of Love My Shepherd Is"

Benediction And Blessing